CARPE THAT F*CKING DIEM

summersdale

CARPE THAT F*CKING DIEM

An Hachette UK Company
www.hachette.co.uk

Summersdale Publishers Ltd
Part of Octopus Publishing Group Limited
Carmelite House
50 Victoria Embankment
LONDON
EC4Y 0DZ
UK

www.summersdale.com

Printed and bound in China

ISBN: 978-1-78685-564-0

Substantial discounts on bulk quantities of Summersdale books are available to corporations, professional associations and other organisations. For details contact general enquiries: telephone: +44 (0) 1243 771107 or email: enquiries@summersdale.com.

TO:

FROM:

"

The envious moment is
flying now, now, while we're
speaking: seize the day.

HORACE

"

WITH THE NEW
DAY COMES NEW
STRENGTH AND
NEW THOUGHTS.

Eleanor Roosevelt

OPPORTUNITIES MULTIPLY AS THEY ARE SEIZED.

SUN TZU

OPEN THE CURTAINS AND LET A NEW F*CKING DAY BEGIN!

Act as if what
you do makes a
difference. It does.

William James

You are never too old
to set another goal or to
dream a new dream.

LES BROWN

IF YOU'RE GOING THROUGH HELL, KEEP GOING.

Anonymous

I'd rather regret the things I've done than regret the things I haven't done.

Lucille Ball

IT'S TIME TO STOP F*CKING AROUND!

If you obey all the rules,
you miss all the fun.

KATHARINE HEPBURN

WHEREVER YOU ARE — BE ALL THERE.

JIM ELLIOT

DIFFICULT DOESN'T MEAN IMPOSSIBLE. EMBRACE THE F*CKING CHALLENGE!

ONE MAY
WALK OVER
THE HIGHEST
MOUNTAIN ONE
STEP AT A TIME.

John Wanamaker

Things do not happen.
Things are made to happen.

JOHN F. KENNEDY

GOOD THINGS COME TO THOSE WHO DON'T F*CKING WAIT

WHO SEEKS SHALL FIND.

Sophocles

IF YOU ASK ME
WHAT I CAME
INTO THIS LIFE
TO DO, I WILL
TELL YOU:
I CAME TO LIVE
OUT LOUD.

Émile Zola

TODAY IS A BLANK PAGE, SO FILL IT WITH BIG SHOUTY CAPITALS!

WHENEVER YOU FALL, <u>PICK</u> <u>SOMETHING UP.</u>

OSWALD AVERY

For myself, I am an optimist – it does not seem to be much use being anything else.

WINSTON CHURCHILL

GET
OFF
YOUR
BACKSIDE!

Tell me, what is it you plan to do with your one wild and precious life?

Mary Oliver

EITHER YOU RUN THE DAY OR THE DAY RUNS YOU.

Jim Rohn

LIFE IS ABOUT TAKING PART – SEIZE THAT F*CKING DAY!

EXPECT PROBLEMS AND EAT THEM FOR BREAKFAST.

ALFRED A. MONTAPERT

I couldn't wait for success,
so I went ahead without it.

Jonathan Winters

Turn your face to the
sun and the shadows
fall behind you.

MAORI PROVERB

To know oneself,
one should
assert oneself.

ALBERT CAMUS

SHOOT
FOR THE
F*CKING
STARS!

I CAN,
THEREFORE
I AM.

Simone Weil

IN ORDER TO SUCCEED, WE MUST FIRST BELIEVE THAT WE CAN.

NIKOS KAZANTZAKIS

BE THE HERO
OF YOUR OWN
FREAKIN' STORY!

You must be the
change you wish to
see in the world.

Mahatma Gandhi

Life is simple –
it's just not easy.

ANONYMOUS

WHAT
ARE YOU
WAITING
FOR?
A F*CKING
INVITATION?

ALL LIFE
IS AN
EXPERIMENT.
THE MORE
EXPERIMENTS
YOU MAKE,
THE BETTER.

Ralph Waldo Emerson

No one knows what
he can do till he tries.

Publilius Syrus

Life is a shipwreck,
but we must not forget
to sing in the lifeboats.

VOLTAIRE

LIFE ISN'T ABOUT FINDING YOURSELF. LIFE IS ABOUT <u>CREATING</u> <u>YOURSELF</u>.

GEORGE BERNARD SHAW

WHETHER YOU
THINK YOU CAN
OR YOU THINK
YOU CAN'T,
YOU'RE RIGHT.

Henry Ford

Do what you can, with what you have, where you are.

THEODORE ROOSEVELT

WHEN YOU REACH THE END OF YOUR ROPE, TIE A KNOT IN IT AND HANG ON.

Anonymous

PERSEVERANCE
IS FAILING
NINETEEN TIMES
AND SUCCEEDING
THE TWENTIETH.

Julie Andrews

SET YOUR GOALS HIGH, AND <u>DON'T</u> <u>STOP TILL YOU</u> <u>GET THERE.</u>

BO JACKSON

The man who removes a mountain begins by carrying away small stones.

CHINESE PROVERB

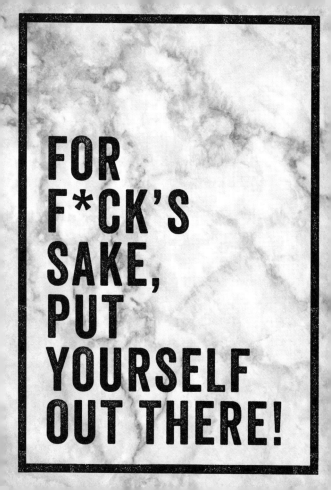

Opportunity does not
knock – it presents
itself when you beat
down the door.

Kyle Chandler

NOTHING IS A WASTE OF TIME IF YOU USE THE EXPERIENCE WISELY.

Auguste Rodin

YOU COULD RUN IN THE RACE, OR F*CKING ORGANIZE IT

IT'S ALWAYS <u>TOO</u> EARLY TO <u>QUIT.</u>

NORMAN VINCENT PEALE

Find ecstasy in life;
the mere sense of
living is joy enough.

Emily Dickinson

QUIT
PROCRASTINATING

If you wait, all that happens
is that you get older.

MARIO ANDRETTI

One joy scatters
a hundred griefs.

CHINESE PROVERB

STILL ON THE SOFA? COME ON, DUDE!

LIFE IS EITHER
A DARING
ADVENTURE
OR NOTHING.

Helen Keller

YOU'RE THE BLACKSMITH OF YOUR OWN HAPPINESS.

SWEDISH PROVERB

SHOW THE WORLD WHAT YOU'RE F*CKING MADE OF!

How wonderful it is that nobody need wait a single moment before starting to improve the world.

Anne Frank

Opportunities are like sunrises. If you wait too long, you miss them.

WILLIAM ARTHUR WARD

MAKE IT
F*CKING
HAPPEN

THERE ARE ALWAYS FLOWERS FOR THOSE WHO WANT TO SEE THEM.

Henri Matisse

It's OK to have butterflies in your stomach. Just get them to fly in formation.

Rob Gilbert

We are all in the gutter
but some of us are
looking at the stars.

OSCAR WILDE

SOME DAYS THERE WON'T BE A SONG IN YOUR HEART. SING ANYWAY.

EMORY AUSTIN

NOTHING WILL
WORK UNLESS
YOU DO.

Maya Angelou

The secret of getting
ahead is getting started.

ANONYMOUS

GET YOUR ASS IN GEAR

THE WISE DOES AT ONCE WHAT THE FOOL DOES AT LAST.

Baltasar Gracián

SETTING GOALS
IS THE FIRST STEP
IN TURNING THE
INVISIBLE INTO
THE VISIBLE.

Tony Robbins

GET OUT THERE AND HAVE SOME F*CKING FUN!

YOU CAN'T TURN BACK THE CLOCK BUT YOU CAN WIND IT UP AGAIN.

BONNIE PRUDDEN

Live today, for tomorrow
it will all be history.

PROVERB

If you can find a path with no obstacles, it probably doesn't lead anywhere.

Frank A. Clark

BE HAPPY. IT'S ONE WAY OF BEING WISE.

Colette

CARPE
THAT DIEM SO
F*CKIN' HARD!

A JOURNEY OF A THOUSAND MILES BEGINS WITH A SINGLE STEP.

LAO TZU

The most important thing is to enjoy your life – to be happy. It's all that matters.

Audrey Hepburn

The best way to predict the future is to create it.

ANONYMOUS

Every artist was
first an amateur.

RALPH WALDO EMERSON

PEDAL TO THE F*CKING METAL!

LIFE SHRINKS
OR EXPANDS IN
PROPORTION TO
ONE'S COURAGE.

Anaïs Nin

THE BEST WAY TO MAKE YOUR DREAMS COME TRUE IS TO WAKE UP.

PAUL VALÉRY

IF AT FIRST
YOU DON'T
SUCCEED, TRY
A-F*CKING-GAIN

I have never met a man
so ignorant that I couldn't
learn something from him.

Galileo Galilei

To me, every hour of the day and night is an unspeakably perfect miracle.

WALT WHITMAN

LIFE IS A HELLUVA LOT MORE FUN IF YOU SAY 'YES' RATHER THAN 'NO'.

Richard Branson

To succeed in life,
you need three things:
a wishbone, a backbone
and a funny bone.

Reba McEntire

Look at life through
the windshield,
not the rear-view mirror.

BYRD BAGGETT

THE BEST WAY OUT IS ALWAYS THROUGH.

ROBERT FROST

LOOK AT
EVERYTHING AS
THOUGH YOU
WERE SEEING IT
FOR THE FIRST
OR LAST TIME.

Betty Smith

"

Nothing really matters
except what you do now
in this instant of time.

EILEEN CADDY

JUST BE YOURSELF: A F*CKING LEGEND

BEGIN TO BE NOW WHAT YOU WILL BE HEREAFTER.

William James

IF YOUR SHIP
DOESN'T COME IN,
SWIM OUT TO IT.

Jonathan Winters

BE WHO
YOU'VE ALWAYS
WANTED TO BE.
BE A F*CKING
ASTRONAUT,
IF YOU WANT!

ATTITUDE IS EVERYTHING.

DIANE VON FÜRSTENBERG

Life begins at the end
of your comfort zone.

NEALE DONALD WALSCH

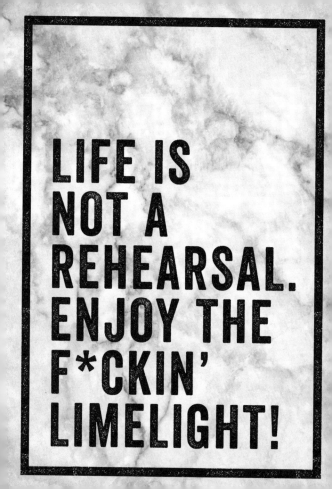

There are exactly as many
special occasions in life as
we choose to celebrate.

Robert Brault

I HAVE
FOUND THAT
IF YOU LOVE
LIFE, LIFE
WILL LOVE
YOU BACK.

Arthur Rubinstein

DON'T WORRY ABOUT TOMORROW – BLOODY WELL ENJOY TODAY!

IF YOU'RE ALREADY WALKING ON THIN ICE, YOU MIGHT AS WELL DANCE.

PROVERB

The most effective way
to do it, is to do it.

Amelia Earhart

You can have anything you
want if you will give up the
belief that you can't have it.

ROBERT ANTHONY

When it is darkest,
men see the stars.

RALPH WALDO EMERSON

YOU CAN'T
EXPECT TO HIT
THE JACKPOT IF
YOU DON'T PUT A
FEW NICKELS IN
THE MACHINE.

Flip Wilson

SHOOT FOR
THE MOON.
EVEN IF YOU
MISS, YOU'LL
LAND AMONG
THE STARS.

LES BROWN

WHEN LIFE
GIVES YOU
LEMONS,
SQUEEZE 'EM
AND ADD
VODKA!

Life isn't about waiting
for the storm to pass;
it's about learning to
dance in the rain.

Anonymous

Change your life today.
Don't gamble on the future,
act now, without delay.

SIMONE DE BEAUVOIR

KNOCK THEIR F*CKING SOCKS OFF

HAPPINESS IS A WAY OF TRAVEL, NOT A DESTINATION.

Roy M. Goodman

Don't get your knickers
in a knot. Nothing
is solved and it just
makes you walk funny.

Kathryn Carpenter

Our greatest glory
is not in never falling,
but in rising every
time we fall.

OLIVER GOLDSMITH

DIFFICULTIES STRENGTHEN THE MIND, AS LABOUR DOES THE BODY.

SENECA THE YOUNGER

NEVER
F*CKING
STOP BEING
A F*CKING
BADASS

FIRST SAY TO
YOURSELF WHAT
YOU WOULD BE;
AND THEN DO
WHAT YOU
HAVE TO DO.

Epictetus

"

Opportunity is missed
by most people because
it is dressed in overalls
and looks like work.

THOMAS EDISON

"

LUCK IS A DIVIDEND OF SWEAT. THE MORE YOU SWEAT, THE LUCKIER YOU GET.

Ray Kroc

DON'T LOAF
AND INVITE
INSPIRATION;
LIGHT OUT AFTER
IT WITH A CLUB.

Jack London

DON'T BE A-F*CKING-FRAID OF GREATNESS!

WHEN YOU COME TO A ROADBLOCK, TAKE A DETOUR.

MARY KAY ASH

The season of failure is
the best time for sowing
the seeds of success.

PARAMAHANSA YOGANANDA

MAKE THIS THE BEST F*CKING DAY EVER!

It's never too late
– never too late to
start over, never too
late to be happy.

Jane Fonda

IF THE WIND WILL NOT SERVE, TAKE TO THE OARS.

Latin proverb

DOORS ARE MADE TO BE OPENED, BUT WALLS ARE MADE TO BE PUSHED THROUGH!

YOU CAN'T USE UP CREATIVITY. THE MORE YOU USE, <u>THE MORE YOU HAVE.</u>

MAYA ANGELOU

It is never too late
to be what you
might have been.

Anonymous

Always be a first-rate version of yourself, instead of a second-rate version of somebody else.

JUDY GARLAND

Whoever is happy will
make others happy too.

ANNE FRANK

A MIND IS LIKE
A PARACHUTE.
IT DOESN'T WORK
IF IT IS NOT OPEN.

Frank Zappa

WITH THE PAST, I HAVE NOTHING TO DO; NOR WITH THE FUTURE. I LIVE NOW.

RALPH WALDO EMERSON

CARPE
THAT
F*CKING
DIEM!

If you're interested in finding out more about our books, find us on Facebook at **Summersdale Publishers** and follow us on Twitter at @Summersdale.

www.summersdale.com